Get Your First Job Using Social Media

10 Stories from
Modern Day Job Seekers

Arthur Lee

Arthur Lee Books
Melbourne, Australia

Copyright © 2022 Arthur Lee

www.arthurlee.com.au

All rights reserved. No part of this book may be reproduced, or stored in a retrieval system, or transmitted in any form or by any means, electronic, mechanical, photocopying, recording, or otherwise, without express written permission of the publisher.

Every effort has been made to trace or contact all copyright holders. The publishers will be pleased to made good any omissions or rectify any mistakes brought to their attention at the earliest opportunity.

ISBN: 9798359362078
Imprint: Independently published

Arthur Lee
PO Box 161, Forest Hill VIC 3131
Australia
ABN: 29 172 617 138

Contents

Subtle Changes Over the Years 1
The freedom that social media brings 3
It's Hard to Get a Job but I Won't Give Up 9
To recruit and to be recruited 15
From social media consumer to creator 21
Always have your wits about you 27
Sales knowledge, patience and consistency 35
Breaking through a sea of applicants 43
Making use of every opportunity 49
Living in the social media space 55
The Hard Road of a Freelancer 61
Afterword 67

Acknowledgements

From top left to bottom right: Athina Caliwara, Dennis Sebuufu, Ella Press, Hamza Hanif, Madhav Regmi, Nnenna Ibeakanma, Ricah Franz, Sovran Hoti, Swathi Nagishetti, Tomas Brein

Subtle Changes Over the Years

When I think of social media as we know it today, it's hard to believe that not long ago, we didn't stare at our phones, tablets or computers for the bulk of our waiting time. It does not seem that long ago that I was sending a text message to a friend during a lecture using my daily 20 free SMS credits, using a phone that only handled eight characters on the screen. It doesn't seem too long ago that I had penpals from different continents, and data for reading emails was very precious. Yet here we are today, a society ruled by social media companies.

We use these platforms for everything, sharing a photo of a proud moment or special occasion, live streaming a video while on holidays, learning on the run, downloading recipes, even binge-watching shows with one eye open at 3 a.m. There is, however, one area that I am not familiar with because I'm a fair way into my career, and that is finding work on social media.

I got my first job from reading an advertisement in the local newspaper, back when there were news articles, classifieds for buying and selling products, notices of sales, declarations of love. The local paper in my area doesn't exist anymore, and only when it disappeared did I realize that, little by little, the traditional paper that I grew up with has now moved onto online spaces in the form of social media.

Although the overall concept of media hasn't changed, using current tools and platforms is very different to what we knew before. Understanding changes can give anyone who is receptive the upper hand.

In this book you will hear different platforms mentioned that we might understand today, but what was amazing when I read the stories is that you can really interchange these brands with whatever new brands pop up in the future.

I asked some questions of 10 people around the world about getting their first job on social media and what wisdom they can offer with finding work in this space. The questions were as follows:

Was it difficult to get a job using social media?

Has work been consistent for you?

Do you think people will increasingly need to look for work through social media?

What words of wisdom can you offer someone looking to get their first job on any social media platform?

I hope you enjoy reading about these people's experiences as they share their story, and if you are looking for work at the moment, then I hope that you can be inspired by the people who did it first.

The freedom that social media brings

Ella Press - Australia

Hello! My name is Ella Press, a full time traveler and (now) digital creator.

I fell in love with travel back in 2019, with a solo backpacking trip around Southeast Asia and Europe, visiting over 30 countries! I returned back to New Zealand just before Covid hit, and after being cooped up at home during the 2020 lockdowns, I got itchy feet and decided that once the borders reopened, I would buy a campervan and embark on a three-month trip around Australia with my partner. I moved to Australia at the end of 2020, and we did exactly that.

During this trip, I started documenting the locations we were visiting around the country on my personal Instagram account, showcasing all of Australia's beauty. Through social media, I befriended a handful of others doing the same, and noticed that they had monetized their accounts to create an income for themselves while they travelled, whether that be through destination photography, tourism boards or collaborating with companies. This gave me the idea to start a brand new account for myself and my partner, with the intention of doing the same. At that time we were living off savings and were interested in finding a way to make money remotely, in hopes of extending our trip for as long as possible.

Naturally over time, the account started to gain a small following on photo and video social media platforms, and we started receiving paid jobs from companies to promote their products and create content for their own advertising. This was a very small sum, but it kept us motivated to continue growing the account and make it worthwhile. A few months in, we decided to invest more money into quality camera gear and a drone, in order to enhance our photography skills and, hopefully, receive more work. Our social media accounts now have 20,000 followers combined, and we have been able to generate a decent income.

Was it difficult to get a job using social media?

In the beginning, it was quite a struggle to grow the account. A lot of trial and error, and attempting to figure it out on my own, as I didn't know anyone personally who I could ask for guidance. Once I researched and implemented new strategies, it was just a matter of consistency. I wasn't quite aware how much of my time it would take just to maintain the account to keep it successful and appealing to companies, so it very much felt like a full-time job with very little pay. There were times that I wanted to call it quits, as I spent every day focussing on running our social media and didn't get to actually enjoy traveling. I figured we had come this far, so I stuck to it as we knew it would be worth it in the long run.

Initially, when working with companies while the account was smaller in size, it was unfortunately quite a negative experience. Due to us being new digital creators, they knew how to take advantage of us;

sneaking extra clauses into contracts, stealing the rights to our content etc, but it was a good learning curve. We have learnt from those rookie errors and were able to then collaborate and create content for some amazing companies.

Has work been consistent for you?

It is definitely not consistent work, as freelancing consistently for one-off jobs can feel like you are constantly trying to stay afloat, due to the income being rather sporadic. It involves a lot of pitching for hours on end, as well as applying for hundreds of jobs through agencies, which can be very time consuming and even devastating as you tend not to receive a reply.

Some companies may not have a budget for content creation through photography, or aren't currently running any specific campaigns that require promotion, so it is very hit and miss. In the beginning, I had little knowledge about where to find these jobs, but over time I have made it a priority to make ourselves known to many marketing agencies, tourism boards and large companies that has resulted in more inbound work. This has been extremely beneficial both in avoiding burnout and time saving.

I am still currently trying to navigate how to use our social media for other sources of income, such as blog writing or affiliate marketing, as if we find success through long term jobs, it will be a lot less exhausting. The ultimate goal is to have the reassurance of knowing we have consistent work and a regular income.

Do you think people will increasingly need to look for work through social media?

Working remotely in general is already increasing, particularly after Covid, and social media is a large portion of that. We are lucky enough that in the new generation we are exposed to a new way of living and the concept of 'ditching the 9-5', as well as companies becoming a lot more open to online workers. We are also moving into a time where an influx of jobs is arising for freelancers, especially social media managers. Social media has changed the way businesses market and engage with their consumers, so there will always be that permanent need of online presence, even in the future.

The aspect of working in social media that I value the most is the ability to work for myself on my own accord, which a large number of people are starting to show interest in, but tend to not know how. As more creators and freelancers are starting to share how this can be an achievable job choice, more people are starting to realize that you don't have to work at an office job if you don't want to, you don't have to stay in a career that you don't enjoy. Especially after a pandemic, the world is coming to a realisation that life is short, and overworking yourself for little return is just not worth it. The more freedom your job gives you, the more time you get to invest into family, friends and experiences.

A word of wisdom for someone looking to get their first job on any social media platform journey

The biggest advice I can give is to just keep pushing through. If you aren't making money instantly, don't quit. If you're finding it difficult to secure a paid job, don't stress. The life that you are working towards won't happen overnight, and that is something that I had to come to terms with early on. The intimidating side of social media is that it can feel oversaturated, and that you're attempting to stand out in a crowd of many, but when 80% of people decide it's too hard for them, you will be the one with the advantage. In the end, the time and effort you invest into landing that job on social media will eventually pay off, and you'll be so glad you stuck to it.

I would also recommend diversifying your options, trying different social platforms, taking free courses and obtaining as much information as you can. A large majority of people who now have jobs through social media started with little knowledge and learnt everything online. Although I still have a long way to go, I can't imagine ever returning to my previous job and giving up the freedom social media has given me. It can be overwhelming to navigate initially, but you won't regret your decision when you start to see it pay off.

It's Hard to Get a Job but I Won't Give Up

Hamza Hanif - Pakistan

Hi, I'm Hamza - a guy who as a child was besotted with the idea of writing his thoughts on a piece of paper. As time went by my love for writing escalated, and soon I found myself writing poetry in multiple languages. I started a page on Instagram.

People loved my work, and soon my page transitioned into something where I could be myself more than in the real world. One of my videos reached 30k views with only 200 followers, however, 7000+ shares baffled me. Long story short, I had to delete that page.

All this sudden attention from my peers was overwhelming for me. I no longer wanted to write for myself, but for others. Soon I figured out that I could pursue content writing as a freelancer. I stumbled upon a certain video online which advised that before starting on professional freelancing platforms, I should build my portfolio by reaching out to clients through social media.

I tried a few social media platforms, and I got my first job on a popular one. I joined as many freelancing groups as I came across using my profile. There I looked every day for relevant jobs, and either directly messaged the person or emailed him/her my proposal. Hence this platform for me became the most comfortable platform to start out as a freelancer.

Was it difficult to get a job using social media?

I must say, indicating finding your first job as difficult would be a serious understatement. It was not a walk in a park. Most people avoid giving jobs to newbies. I created a portfolio website, wrote sample articles, and never stopped sending proposals.

After some time, I realized that I was not messaged back even by a single client after sending hundreds of proposals. I figured out that I needed to stand out from the immense competition. I tried every trick in the book, and every time I was more disappointed than ever by these silent rejections. Somehow, I never stopped even though I wanted to…really badly. I promised myself that I would stop counting the proposals I had been sending and let my luck play out through consistency.

Finally, after months of work, I not only got a reply but my first client too. After working so much for this, I could not have been happier. I spent all day working on that article and did my best. I added statistics, facts, and photos to make it more engaging. It is safe to say that I gave it my all. Luckily the client liked my work. He gave me another job the same day. However, there were some communication problems at that time that made it really hard for me to get feedback on how the articles were performing. I never figured out what blog the client owned, and where my articles were being published. Hence there were both positive and negative aspects to this experience.

Has work been consistent for you?

Consistent…not really. As I was not credited for the articles or provided any links to them being published, my portfolio stayed the same. The only thing I got was real-time experience, which is actually highly precious.

Now I know that if you knock on a thousand doors, one of them will definitely open up. I trusted God and kept on trying. I learned that by being hopeless I was just letting myself down. Also, I started it as a hobby and nothing more, which made me love the process even more.

I was not pressured to do anything; it was just something that made me realize how much I loved writing. Believing in myself, I made an account on a popular freelancing platform. I tried the same techniques that I tried on social media, and guess what? It took me much more time to get my first client here. I doubt that I could have endured this much disappointment if I was not taught by experience on social media.

Hence, it is undoubtedly a struggle, but that is what keeps it engaging for me. If I got everything easy, I would never be able to measure its worth. I am climbing up the ladder slowly but surely.

Do you think people will increasingly need to look for work through social media?

In my opinion, social media will continue to rise further. As it is more familiar to use, there is a huge demand for freelancers out there. I believe the right portfolio ensures great clients. A portfolio is not built in a day, and everything happens systematically. Even top-rated freelancers on professional platforms are more open to jobs outside as there are not many restrictions, plus you get more creative freedom. As these professional platforms attract clients through social proof, a single bad rating can destroy a freelancer's career. On social media, however, you have enough control. This does not mean one should misuse it or overpromise. It is just a way out for a freelancer who got an unfair rating somehow, as what to show on social media is up to him/her.

Due to these reasons, I am inclined to believe that finding work through social media will increase over time. There are no barriers to entry or exit, and the huge demand for freelancers makes some skills highly worthwhile to learn and apply. It is both a good learning platform and a place to find your best long-term clients.

A word of wisdom for someone looking to get their first job on any social media platform

There are two things that you can be sure of. First, you will be rejected countless times so be ready for that. Second, if you are talented, hardworking, and consistent enough you will find jobs eventually. As your client base increases over time, work your best to improve your portfolio, and ask for credit politely if the client is comfortable. Do ask permission from the client on whether you can show others the work you have done for him/her as a sample.

Only apply to relevant jobs and be open to learning and improving each day. Also, be honest with your work, never misguide anyone and be open to corrections or revisions. You must build trust between yourself and the client, but never fake it. Do it genuinely, it is so much easier.

Remember, more is always better. Do not leave a single social media platform, you never know what will work for you. You might need to make some compromises on the first few jobs, but everything gets better over time.

The most important thing is to never lose hope and always believe in yourself, because if you don't, then how can people trust you with the jobs? So always deliver more than promised. Stay motivated and keep grinding. Success may be far away, but you will reach it.

Good luck!

To recruit and to be recruited

Athina Caliwara - Qatar

My name is Athina. I am currently working as a human resource management and marketing professional here in Doha, Qatar. With a bachelor's degree in advertising and public relations, I have gathered more than 12 years of cross-functional experience both in human resource management and marketing.

In 2014, I successfully landed a recruitment consultant role for a global recruitment company through a social media platform for professionals. As an HR professional, talent acquisition and recruitment are two of my core skills. Usually, our pool of talents comes from direct applicants (website and walk-ins) or through job portals. During that time, there was one social media platform for professionals that was starting to make its name in recruitment. I tried this platform because everyone was suggesting that I use it to search for new job opportunities.

During that time this platform great, because the feeds on job posts are all corporate or business related. I have also noticed that employers locally and internationally are proactively posting a wide range of job opportunities. I explored the platform and realised that I should invest in strengthening my professional profile or portfolio to attract employers and to be shortlisted on my applications. I would apply to more than 10 employers in a day and would get interviews in the same week. After getting competitive offers, I took my applications on this platform more seriously until I landed the opportunity as a recruitment consultant.

Was it difficult to get a job using social media?

It was one of the most challenging interviews I ever had. Since the HR team which contacted me is not locally based, it took me some time to take their instructions seriously. Getting the job was smooth and easy but to be selected for this opportunity, I needed to take some risks. Pushing through with my application was a leap of faith for me.

They initially conducted a telecom interview and when I got selected, they required me to travel to Dubai. Although it was an all-expenses-paid trip, it was a risk for a single woman like me to travel to another country just to go through a one-day screening. Everyone was discouraging me from going because it seemed too good to be true. They all thought it was a complete online fraud. Fortunately, it was totally legitimate and to date is the most challenging and nerve-racking screening experience I ever had.

All candidates were required to complete one full day of screening process which, I must admit, was difficult but was very satisfying to pass. The entire experience was positive in all aspects - the company compensation, benefits, work environment and overall management was above average and was very competitive to the market during that time.

Has work been consistent for you?

During the first few months, every phase was very exciting. The job required me to travel a lot during training and all my batchmates and I have a lot of opportunities for our personal and career development. We all get to meet a lot of different people coming from various industries in different countries.

However, as the training went on, I realized that the job includes selling. Basically, we need to approach potential companies to get job requirements and develop existing client requirements. In short, aside from recruiting, we also need to sell the service. I am a very diligent person, I learn new things quickly and will always seek to be on top of my game and work with excellence but, unfortunately, selling is not part of my skill-set - and obviously, the job requires a lot of it.

I also learned that my job offer was different from the job offer of my seniors as I came from a different hiring program. I must admit it was not a very successful part of my career as I was not able to reach my target KPIs and I was personally feeling frustrated about it. I officially started in January 2015 and ended my contract exactly 12 months after joining.

Do you think people will increasingly need to look for work through social media?

We are currently in a time where everything gets done digitally online. With social media continuously developing to provide our daily necessities, there is no doubt that finding jobs through social media will continue to increase. Social media can easily develop programs that will customise the needs of both the jobseekers and headhunters.

As a recruiter myself, social media has helped me a lot in directly reaching my target talents in different roles. A post on a social media platform can go a long way. In my most recent job where I was working as a marketing and admin executive for a group of companies, I handled the department in charge of social media. One of the objectives was to grow our organic followers on every platform.

As I also work as an assistant to the Group Operations Manager who assigns me to spearhead specific job roles, I have strategically used the social media platform for professionals to assist me in both of my roles. A job posting there will attract hundreds of potential candidates who will also add to my organic following and will create traffic to our digital platforms - so I don't just get to find the suitable candidate, I also get to add organic followers to our official social media pages.

On the other hand, as a jobseeker, I think it's worth mentioning that we should also be careful with job opportunities through social media. We should verify the source of the job opportunities before applying.

Get Your First Job Using Social Media

What word of wisdom can you offer someone looking to get their first job on any social media platform

Social media is the most convenient way to land a job. From the comfort of your home, you can process applications in a few clicks. There are a lot of opportunities waiting for us but, unfortunately, it's also an open ground for fraud. Some employers are even advertising job titles for a totally different role, so it is very important to read the job descriptions carefully.

To avoid turning your dream job into a nightmare, you first need to verify the authenticity of the source. From the person who posted it to the name of the organization, to whether the account has been verified as a legitimate institution or corporation, you need to make sure that the job posting is legitimate.

Secondly, make sure you understand the job requirements and qualifications and make sure that your qualifications comply with it before proceeding with your application. It would be a waste of time for both you and the employer to process your applications, only to realize that you are unfit for the role, or the job is not within your scope.

Last but not least, invest in strengthening your portfolio. Make sure that all your core skills are highlighted in your profile. Aside from job opportunities, social media has also made it possible for us to learn easily and conveniently and strengthen our qualifications through online certifications, online courses and a lot of personal and career development courses.

From social media consumer to creator

Tomas Brein - Argentina

My name is Tomas Brein, I am a law student at the University Torcuato Di Tella in Argentina. As a result of going to a bilingual school, I am proficient in both English and Spanish. I am a passionate researcher and blog writer with a profound sense of identity towards the activities and jobs I take part in.

I successfully found work on a photo and video based social platform. I managed an account on self-growth and financial freedom, uploading posts and talking to clients and providers. I also found work writing two different blogs on self-growth on two different websites. Like every person who shares their lives with others and stays connected with others, I ended up on Instagram. The key difference is that I developed a great interest in accounts that offer other people their management and development from this platform

Thus, I ended up expressing interest in some of them and finally getting contacted to work on the management of one of these accounts, and later, on the publishing of blog posts for the websites of other different accounts. I believe I ended up here by having a hustling mindset and being an ambitious person who does not settle and constantly looks for interesting opportunities to learn while working.

Was it difficult to get a job using social media?

It was not difficult to get the job itself. If anything could be considered difficult from the process I took part of, it is shifting the mindset from consumer to creator. The toughest part of getting the job was to begin contacting different accounts and proposing my services to them. By the momentum I built from sending my first proposal, it became easier each time I did it until I finally found a job that interested me, benefited my client and also benefited me in learning this new growing type of work.

It was a very positive experience for me. The main reason for this is that understanding this whole new branch of opportunities that social media brings with them is a great step towards learning how to work in a way which is very different to what most people believe is the only way. Actually having found work on social media and working on something inside of it such as the community management of an account illustrates and proves to be true the immense specter of possibilities they bring. Thus, I believe at least at an early age everyone should be looking forward to doing so, as it is a fascinating experience as to what it represents and how it can lead you to a great shift in mindset.

Has work been consistent for you?

As I have had different jobs found on social media, the consistency differs in each of them. It all depends on one great factor, the sense of identity the job brings to you and your passion for it. Only the last job I started, as a personal development blog writer, was consistent - the others have not been as consistent. I struggled with the habit of putting in the work mainly as a result of not feeling I was learning in the process, and it did not feel appropriate for me. As I did not feel the passion needed to work as I do now, it was much more difficult to do it consistently.

So, finding a job on social media is not only about how difficult it may be to get one but also about how consistent it is in itself and how consistently you can put in your best passionate work in order for it to be a positive experience. I find the variety of topics and freedom in writing or working in your own way to be two key factors when evaluating how consistent the work can be for you. Personally, I believe it is imperative for you to be passionate about what you do and have the feeling that it helps not just you but others, by contributing to a greater mission or objective.

Once I found the right work for me, it was not a struggle anymore and I no longer needed to put in a great effort to do the work. My journey has been as simple as contacting different accounts and accepting jobs in order to try them out and get to know this industry and myself better. When I finally found one that aligned perfectly with my personality, I kept on doing it up to this day.

Do you think people will increasingly need to look for work through social media?

I believe it will increase for many reasons - principally, because more and more businesses have a social media account. Think about it, there are more local businesses every day that grow their audience and publicise themselves on social media. Think of all the possible jobs these businesses create as they need people to manage their communities by answering messages and uploading posts. There are also many entrepreneurs that look for people to manage their accounts and clients. Moreover, it is easier to contact potential workers through social media where there is less friction than in a traditional job offer.

Finding work through social media will also increase as a result of how many people use the different platforms and there are more and more of them who understand the search algorithms and the most effective way to run social accounts. As there is not only a growing demand but an increasing supply in this job market, each party involved can benefit, thus resulting in a sustained growth of finding work through social media. It will become more common each day to hear that this is happening and to know people who work on community management on social media accounts or are reached out to via direct messages to do some other related work.

A word of wisdom for someone looking to get their first job on any social media platform:

Take action without fear of failure. It is better to start contacting businesses now than to procrastinate, to learn during the process and show willingness to learn and work hard. Once I understood this and started sending my proposals to every account I saw as suitable for myself, getting the first job became much easier, and so did finding the right one. We tend to build a resistance inside our minds that prevents us from doing what we want. This resistance may be a result of different possible factors such as perfectionism, fear of failure or others.

The ultimate truth is, this feeling will not go away with time or further planning: you need to take action, to take a simple first step. With that in mind, do not let anything stop you, reach for your desired outcomes and they will come by themselves with positive thinking. It took me quite some time to understand this and act upon it, but when I finally did, I saw the whole picture. By looking back on my journey, I can tell you to hope for the best in your own trajectory, do not procrastinate any longer and take action right now.

Always have your wits about you

Ricah Franz - United Arab Emirates

You can call me Ricah or, as my friends love to call me, Cai. I am currently a social media and marketing executive at a local sporting events company. I mainly handle all the social media accounts of the business along with its five other subsidiary brands. I pride myself in everything that I do and most importantly my job.

The previous retail company I was working with shut down during the peak of the COVID-19 pandemic. I was one of the many career-driven-turned-jobless people who lost their bread and butter almost instantaneously…who also happened to struggle to find a job in a competition ten times bigger than usual.

It's funny how I used to believe that there are certain job sites where you will find professional work, you know, the "big leagues" – any other platforms are just some Ponzi schemes ready to ask me to carry out a suspicious job. On a more serious note, I also made myself believe that I had what it takes to contend against a pool of people who are all just trying to survive the sudden recession. And that, 1.) I would be headhunted and 2.) the job will find its way to me so very easily but boy, was I wrong. I received countless turndowns that made me rethink my capabilities as a person. It made me wonder if I was someone who can bring something to the table or if my confidence was mere naivety.

After being laid off for eight months, I was ready to pop the bubble in my head and re-calibrate my job-hunting strategies. The constant rejections finally made me turn to job groups, communities, and sections in every social media platform–which I was still cynical about at the time. Nevertheless, I continued my path down the rabbit hole and into a traditional social networking platforms's now-gone job section and, lo and behold, I found the job that saved my expat life and downward-spiralling career.

Was it difficult to get a job using social media?

Given the fact that I lost my previous job at the time of the pandemic (which I now know was far from over), the job-hunting experience was rather difficult than it would normally be.

One good thing about it, though, was the Internet. I wouldn't have been able to survive if it weren't for the online opportunities I was presented with at the time. I would say that it's a rather neutral experience than an entirely negative or positive one. Because, despite what seem to be favorable chances in the online world, along with it are employers who are not just taking advantage of the desperate applicants but also outrageously low-balling us.

I have had employers ask me if they can keep me under probation for a month or so without providing any benefits, despite it being a 9-5 full-time job. I also had an employer who wanted to keep me permanently for the job but pay me as little as $100 for the entire month. Another employer expected me to agree to do the work-from-home setup but would not provide the most basic tool required, a computer.

Apart from the ridiculous offers, the communication part was also something that made the job search even more difficult for me. As a Millennial, the vibe of the people I am going to work with and the overall environment is something I consider vital. Before the boom of video conferencing, all parts of the interview would be conducted over a phone-call, email, or chat... and I haven't got the faintest idea what kind of person is on the other side of the line. I am an extremely expressive person, and that trait helps me converse and market myself significantly. The lack of face-to-face meetings for a while was also one of the many frustrations I had in getting a job.

Fortunately, the job I found on social media required a personal interview shortly after an exchange of emails. When asked how I found their listing, I honestly answered that their masked email looked like a fake company posing as a legitimate one, but I was optimistic and so I applied. Two days later, they called me back to inform me that I got the job, and the rest is history.

Has work been consistent for you?

Since I got the job through Facebook, things have been pretty steady for me.

To be honest, up to this day I still cannot believe that I found a secure position in a well-established firm with great benefits in the last place I considered looking for a job.

I have been working for the same company since 2020 and I was not even once considered for a cut despite external factors that could cause my employer to issue layoffs or downsize. I consider this experience as one of the greatest times when my negative prejudices were proved wrong.

Do you think people will increasingly need to look for work through social media?

The big shift caused by the pandemic made social media one of the most powerful tools not only for communication but for an array of other things like job-searching. Communities and groups have been built for the sole purpose of helping people find jobs without expecting anything in return. It has been a give-and-take situation for everyone inside these caring communities.

Interestingly, it has also been a way to confirm whether a company or an interview invite is legitimate or just a waste of time. I tried to authenticate a few freelance jobs here and there through these groups. I also try to give back the favor by posting relevant job listings, interviewing tips, and even making editable CV templates for free.

Taking all things into consideration, I believe job-hunting will never go back to the traditional way. Apart from the accessible recruitment tools online, social media has played a fascinating part in terms of looking for a job and it will certainly flourish even more over time. I, for one, know that when it's time for me to look for growth and change my career in the future, I will primarily scour these platforms before heading to what I used to refer to as the "big leagues".

A word of wisdom for someone looking to get their first job on any social media platform

As you went through my story, I am certain that I have mentioned my skepticism about getting a job through social media at least twice. Although I may have managed to find a four-leaf clover and get lucky with my job-hunting experience through social media, there are a lot of things I have also considered when looking for a job in the digital world.

Some of the main things, or warning signs rather, that I look out for are the job listing composition, the requirements, and the company name. "Why these three", you ask? This is because the hiring department must always uphold and be in line with the reputation and voice of the company. Sure, this may not be the case for every business, firm or company but those three are the most basic guidelines for putting out a vacancy in public.

Composition: You may want to think twice when a job listing is poorly written, and full of grammatical mistakes and punctuation errors. It should be clear and easy to understand, and that means that there can't be any typographical error or two. Professional companies wouldn't let that kind of PR nightmare fly.

Requirements: Think about what you're applying for and press the job requirements against it. If you are applying for a Commis Chef, for example, and they are asking for a whole-body picture, a close-up, and a picture of your feet, you may want to pass up on this.

Company: Information is widely available nowadays. Everything you need, want, and don't want to know is just right at your fingertips. If you research for a company and it comes up empty or you read a few 'stay away from this' reviews, please consider it as an early warning sign. A legal company or recruiter can be found in at least one out of a handful of social media platforms —especially when they are using one to hire their next star employees.

Social media, when used wisely, is a very powerful tool but the bitter truth is that it's also a double-edged sword. Everyone is taking it to their advantage with little to no regard for others. Likewise, you may want to use it to find a job that will head-start your career but keep in mind that there will also be *a lot* of people who are ready to put out bait for the next perfect job search scam. It's always smart to equip yourself with a little bit of common sense and not be afraid to ask questions as necessary when using social media for anything. Take it from me, I live and breathe social media 24/7, 365.

Sales knowledge, patience and consistency

Madhav Regmi - Nepal

I am Madhavam from Nepal, and I have successfully found jobs on a few social media platforms.

I started with a theme page on a photo and video sharing platform inspired by online videos on it. Luckily, someone approached me the day I created the page, and I got my first mentor in the field. With their one on one mentorship, I learned that there are many things to know and personal mentorship can help a lot. While my first mentorship was running, I got an offer from another mentor for mentorship on these theme pages and sales. Since it was something I was interested in and I had experienced great value from the first mentorship, I instantly joined the second mentorship. And, by the grace of God, this mentorship went unexpectedly well. I got to dive into the knowledge of sales, which changed my vision entirely. It made me believe that we can do almost anything when we understand it.

After my mentorships, I started finding clients with whom I could work. Only seventeen days after joining my first mentorship, I got my first client in social media mentorship. I started working with them and it continued. Today, I have worked with six students, with more than a dozen brands in content services (infographics and reels), and with two brands as a social media account manager. My knowledge of sales helped me to convince them to have me do their job.

Later, I expanded to other popular social media platforms. As a student of software engineering, I currently work in web development and web designing. I am currently working with one startup as a web developer, whom I got from a messenger app. Being also fond of writing, I am working with multiple brands in paid article-writing.

To explain how I ended up on the other platforms - I paused working on my initial social media page. Due to this, it became inactive and finding businesses to work with has been challenging. I will return to it soon, making a robust and active network that will help me approach businesses easily for work and deals. Talking about the messaging services, they are currently running actively. I am working on web development, web designing, and article writing.

Was it difficult to get a job using social media?

Since I got to have two mentorships in the early stage of starting my journey with theme pages on the photo and video sharing social media site, I learned how we should move to make money using it. I utilized the knowledge to approach different brands and businesses. Out of hundreds of brands that I came to, I got to work with tens of them up to now, only from this single social media platform.

While approaching businesses and being rejected multiple times, directly or indirectly, it was hard to maintain hope that I would also get the opportunity to work with brands on social media platforms, but I managed to keep my patience anyhow. So I successfully got my first client for my social media mentorship; I worked with a brand to develop and establish their business on a social media platform. Getting the first payment in advance inspired me to do more. Except for defending the rejections, accepting them, and being patient, I did not find other parts as complex in getting jobs through social media - this is because of implementing my proper sales knowledge.

It was a positive experience for me, as I was able to deal with different brands and difficulties on the way. I was finally able to know how everything works in making money online and the psychology of people. I finally learned and accepted the highs and lows on the path and used them to further my path. And, since I implemented the same sales knowledge in convincing businesses on messaging services, I didn't find any difficulties with those platforms as I already had good experience dealing with everything required. Overall, it is an excellent and sweet experience for me to be in this online working field.

Has work been consistent for you?

When I started with the Instagram theme page and got mentorships, I understood that being consistent will make you succeed in your targets. And that is why I tried to be consistent, and I have worked for around a year on Instagram. I started consistently providing value to people and showing my expertise through content on my social media page, which functioned as my portfolio in terms of values.

Talking more about my portfolio, I used to provide some of my services for free to some brands and collect testimonials from them, which worked as a part of my portfolio in terms of the work I could do. This helped me impress other brands so I could finally make paid deals with brands. After I got to work with different brands with paid sales, the payment proofs and testimonials from them created me a strong portfolio, which made it much easier for me to present my ideas to brands so I could convince them to hire me to do their job correctly.

As long as I was consistent on my social media page, I could easily keep things going, but when I paused the activity on my Instagram feed, the active audience I used to have started to decrease over time . Even though it was falling, I was already connected to some brands, whom I used to talk to via Instagram direct messages, and I could manage to work with a few more brands from there. However, with time and my inactivity on Instagram, I could not make deals with new businesses. When the interactions with old brands ended, I stopped getting more jobs via Instagram. From here, I learned that we should not be inactive on social media profiles where we do business with others. This can result in a sudden downfall in the graph of your active networks, connections, audiences, contracts, and incomes. I learned that being inconsistent can lead you to the struggling phase again if you are working on the foundation of any social media profiles.

Do you think people will increasingly need to look for work through social media?

I believe that finding work through social media will increase over time because of the increasing population, competition over their physical locations for jobs, growing unemployment over time, the craze and trend of working remotely, and the inspiration from those who successfully work and have businesses online.

Over time, it is becoming difficult for people to turn their academic careers into cash flow, and the unemployment rate is increasing. Many people studying in academics or preparing for competitive exams are seeing people finding it difficult to get jobs. This impacts their psychology with them not having or being able to gain employment or cracking the competitive exams for jobs.

Extending this, nowadays, entities recruiting people for positions are focusing on the skills that they have rather than the degrees they possess. This impacts and inspires people of different mindsets to find the alternative or to develop skills that will make them stand out and find a job much more easily, as academic degrees are losing their value over time when it comes to recruiting staff.

Finding work through social media will increase with entities looking to hire people who can do their job with the best quality, no matter where they work. This remote-working style will increase over time with the internet and technology.

A word of wisdom for someone looking to get their first job on any social media platform

My word of wisdom for anyone looking to get their first job on any social media platform starts with saying to know how the system works in the project you're on – see how the social media works, how you can utilise it, and what are the requirements you need to accomplish your targets/projects. Knowing how the particular social media platform works, how to utilize it, and the requirements you need is not a very hard task for anyone.

The information is available both online and offline, free of charge or paid. You just need to research to find out everything and implement the right ways to successfully achieve what you want. This applies to both businesses and jobs, online and offline. Remember that a paid method is not a must for anyone but can accelerate things if you get suitable materials or mentors.

In this digital world, anyone can build a business in the right way. It can be the right approach for jobs and good pitching for businesses. And, for this, you can learn about sales that will teach you how human psychology works, how to approach people or companies, and how to pitch and convince them. I always recommend people to learn sales as it is not only a skill of selling things but more of convincing people to do anything.

Imagine if you could easily convince anyone to provide you with a job, do business with you, or even increase your salary. Wouldn't it be fantastic? –

Definitely, YES! That is why sales is a master skill that anyone should have, in my opinion. This also works in building solid relationships with anyone and with the recruiter in the case of getting a job. Furthermore, with sales skills, you can learn how to express or present anything to anyone so you can stand out of the crowd and get detected easily. It supports your copywriting, speaking, and leadership abilities and makes strong relationship bonds with anyone, and convinces them. I believe that with all these skills, you can get your first job quickly on any social media platform. I congratulate you in advance on your first job from a social media platform!

Breaking through a sea of applicants

Nnenna Okeke - Nigeria

My name is Nnenna Ibeakanma Okeke, a Nigerian and the last child from a middle-class family of seven. I am married with four children. I am a law graduate from Nnamdi Azikiwe University and was called to the Nigerian bar in 2010. Immediately after my call to the bar, I joined a law firm and went into full time law practice and litigation. Sometime in 2020, there was a total lockdown in my country as a result of Coronavirus that hit the world and this drastically affected livelihoods as people were asked to stay indoors to reduce the spread of the virus.

My quest to earn a living to sustain my family made me explore the internet and I realized that the social media we use on a daily basis can be a source of income if utilized well.

One fateful day, I came across a job post on social media platform for a social media manager, who would assist in getting real and organic subscribers to subscribe to and engage with a video channel. I quickly sent a message in the comment section indicating my interest. The job poster requested a proposal and I sent a convincing proposal stating that I belong to an online community of thousands of people that can help me achieve the goal. That was how my freelancing journey began from social media and I have expanded to other social media platforms and freelance sites.

Was it difficult to get a job using social media?

I would say that getting the job was quite difficult because on the comment section of the job post, so many people indicated interest in the job role and the job poster also dropped a reply on over 300 of such comments asking for a proposal, just as he did on my comment.

After sending the proposal, it took him one week to acknowledge my proposal and drop a reply informing me that there will be stages of interview before selection. I perceived that the delay in response was due to the large number of proposals he received.

The interview was a very difficult and rigorous process for me, being that I had little or no experience in social media management. There were three stages of the interview. The first stage was basic questions on the knowledge ads of a popular video site, as well as icons and views. The second stage of the interview was to make a pitch video on a video platform selling myself and my abilities. The third and the final stage of the interview was getting hundred persons to view and like my pitch video within thirty minutes. Going through these processes wasn't easy considering the fact that I was new to the system. Even though I finally got the job, I experienced difficulties in trying to sell myself to the client.

Not giving up on the job was a positive experience, because I learnt a whole lot from the interview process and I gained more exposure from executing the task.

Has work been consistent for you?

It has been consistent work for me. However, my consistency has been by referrals, mostly from my very first client. The journey so far has been filled with ups and downs. This is because there are times I submit proposals without getting a response and during these times, one will ordinarily feel like giving up. There are also times I submit proposals and get job offers, and those times, I appreciate the fact that I did not give up.

Do you think people will increasingly need to look for work through social media?

With the sudden rise of remote working, finding work through social media will certainly be on the increase over time. This is because the era of carrying files from one company to the other in search of jobs is gradually phasing out. Companies now utilize social media sites for marketing and promoting their businesses and also for recruitment purposes as they find it easier locating potential candidates for their job positions on social media.

It is no secret that the younger generations are now engrossed in social media and that everything they do revolves around it, including searching for and finding jobs.

The list of jobs that can be found on social media is inexhaustible. Such jobs include data entry, proofreading, social media management, virtual assistant, customer care services, graphic design, artificial intelligence, transcription etc. This is a clear indication that there are more remote jobs than on-site jobs.

Also, research has shown that employers feel more comfortable using social networking sites to research candidates for jobs. This means that employers get a clearer picture of who their prospective employees are apart from what their resume portrays them to be, through social media sites.

In conclusion, finding work on social media has come to stay and grow on a daily basis because there is no limit to the kind of jobs that could be found on social media - either fixed jobs, contract jobs or long term.

A word of wisdom for someone looking to get their first job on any social media platform:

Searching for and getting a first job role on any social media platform is usually not easy, but with the 'Grit and Growth' mindset, one will pull through. Rejections will definitely come because hirers will be skeptical to hire, seeing that the person is on entry-level - but how you handle it is what matters most.

Sometimes, we may be discouraged and tempted to believe that only lucky people receive the best opportunities. However, numerous opportunities can come to anyone regardless of sex, age and race, when we unrelentingly put in the hard work.

I would encourage a beginner to adopt the following job success principles:

Don't give up. After submitting proposals and your resume on social media for job roles without a response from a job recruiter, don't feel the need to stop. Rather, go back to your previous proposals and try to identify where you are not getting it right, amend them and change your pattern.

Be consistent and persistent. Consistency in the job search and the submission of proposals will not only help in improving your proposal pattern but will eventually land you your first job and other jobs consequently.

Believe in yourself. Having confidence in yourself will place you at a better angle to sell yourself to employers and also, boost your morale. Also, believing in yourself gives you the confidence you need to successfully deliver 100% on the job after landing your first role.

Making use of every opportunity

Dennis Sebuufu - Uganda

I'm Dennis Sebuufu, a freelance copywriter and translator from Uganda. I tried various avenues to make money online without success until I joined a popular social media platform. Before this social media platform gained popularity, I was on a few others. These worked differently and didn't have as many features as this one. For example, they didn't have groups and pages.

One social network I was on before joining this particular platform would allow creating a profile and chatting with friends. When this social media craze reached my country over seven years ago, I did not hesitate to sign up. At first, I would only log in to chat with friends. It was a whole new experience with various features like joining groups of people with similar interests or liking a page of a brand you admire.

After some time, I discovered that I could actually make money through the platform. I started by joining marketing groups where I would sell my products. Later, I came across some groups for people working online from other countries. It crossed my mind that there was a lot more to this social platform than just selling products to people in my area and chatting with friends.

I became more interested in the freelancer groups and joined as many as I could. These introduced me to various people across the globe who have been instrumental in my freelancing career for the last six years.

Was it difficult to get a job using social media?

Like any other platform where people search for jobs, it's the same on social media. Other freelancers are looking out for job opportunities like you. Getting my first job on the social platform seemed like a fairy tale. In one of my freelance writers' groups, I came across a lady looking for someone to write ebooks for her. She was based in the US. The ebooks were about biographies of real-life serial killers.

I never thought twice when I told her I would handle the task despite not having experience as a freelance online copywriter. The lady game let me write the ebooks for her without asking about my experience. I think it was not difficult to get the job back then since there weren't many freelancers on the prowl for opportunities like today.

Getting my first writing job on social media was a positive experience. I realized I could make money as a freelance writer and work for people worldwide. A chance to write for her and liking my work made me realise that I'm a great writer! On a sad note, I never got to receive my payment from her because of difficulties with the mode of payment. However, after that experience, I didn't hesitate to keep searching for freelance writing work through the platform.

Has work been consistent for you?

From my experience, I would say getting jobs on social media has been consistent. I have never missed a week without earning through the platform. I have worked for years with some of the clients I got on social media. My freelance writing journey has been amazing. I have worked with people from different parts of the world. Some had never heard of my country! I have built meaningful relations with the people I have worked for on the platform. Some even recommend me to their friends and other business owners.

I even used to write product reviews for a client whose payment I would earn in a week from other clients. He would pay me a quarter of his wage for my services. An interesting bit about the relationship with my social media clients is that we don't switch to other means of communication. After writing, I drop document links in the messaging service for them to send and confirm they have sent my payment. Luckily, this social media network no longer treats them as spam like when I had just started.

I can't spend an hour without logging in since I look forward to a text from any of my clients on the messaging service at any time. Apart from freelance writing, I also discovered a need for translators in my local language through its groups. Thanks to this platform, I developed two skills that have become my primary source of income.

Do you think people will increasingly need to look for work through social media?

I don't think finding work through social media is going to decrease. Thanks to the pandemic, more people spend time on social media platforms today than ever. This has caught the attention of hiring managers looking for new hires. So, they post vacancies in their organizations on their social media pages. People looking for jobs are always keeping a close eye on the pages of companies they want to work for.

Finding work through social media will increase over time because it's very convenient for job-seekers who don't have to spend time elsewhere to find opportunities. Someone can browse through posts on their favorite social media platform and find a job post from a company they have always wanted to work for.

Many brands have a strong presence on social media since they want to be where their potential customers spend their time. The brands hire dedicated social media managers to keep their pages updated with new products or services and job opportunities. No wonder hiring managers may also check out what applicants post on their social media accounts to choose the best for the position.

Overall, finding work on social media is going to continue growing. More and more companies appreciate its relevance in reaching out to people who are genuinely interested in their brands.

Get Your First Job Using Social Media

A word of wisdom for someone looking to get their first job on any social media platform

Anyone looking to get their first job on any social media platform should be wise when choosing a platform to find potential employers. Different categories of employers use particular social platforms and more corporate brands use other platforms.

You should also join groups relevant to your industry or profession. If you're a freelance writer, search for groups with other freelance writers and join. Here, you will meet like-minded professionals, some of whom may have a vacancy in their organization at some point. There's also a chance to network with people in the same profession and discuss ways to get more opportunities.

Another idea to see you land your first client on a social platform is to follow the brands you want to work for. Look for their accounts on social platforms and like their pages. This will keep you aware of whatever is happening. If there's an open position, hiring managers are likely to share it on the platform. You will know about the vacancy before others see it elsewhere, such as in newspaper ads.

Social platforms are hotbeds of all kinds of work if you know how to get it. Join as many platforms as you can and follow your favorite brands. You will always know whenever there's an open position.

Living in the social media space

Swathi Nagishetti - India

Hi, I'm Swathi, I'm from India. My hobbies are reading and cooking. Here I am sharing my job hunt and success experience: In 2018, I started my photo and video sharing social media account. I had started posting some random quotes and pictures on the account by using relevant hashtags. Until that time, I had no intention of applying for jobs on Instagram and I have no idea about that process.

Gradually I started getting some followers. Also, a few contest freaks were tagging me in their contest entry, which increased my profile visibility. After a few days, I updated my profile picture with an original picture to participate in contests that are hosted by brands and businesses. I started participating in contests. After 15 days I had won three contests and two giveaways. I was very happy and got a good network as well. I won more contests eventually and brands started reaching out to me for collaborations.

One day, I was scrolling through a social media platform and I found an advertisement like "Hiring a Social Media Manager for Giveaway Hosting". I was very interested in that job and applied for it. Though I was not selected for that job, it gave me a good interview experience. After a few months, I revamped my entire profile and made it a social media manager profile. I started posting about social media management, social media-related content, and freelancer-related contests on my profile. Slowly my network increased. I even started cold messaging to different brands and businesses.

One day, I received a reply from a client in the United Kingdom saying that she wanted to hire a social media manager to manage her small business page. I was so excited and immediately replied to her saying that I will set up a video conference and discuss starting the project further. We interacted at the meeting and she was very happy with my portfolio and offered me the contract to manage her page. This is my first job on a social media platform. I have completed my fourth month with this client and she is so happy with the results. This is how I landed my first job on social media.

Was it difficult to get a job using social media?

I would say it is more challenging. It was not difficult but it was challenging. The job-hunting process had ups and downs. Initially, I sent many cold messages to many brands but none of them opened my message. Then I started closely following the brand, interacting with their posts regularly, reposting their stories and occasionally promoting their brand on my stories.

This initiative captured their attention, and a few brands offered me small part-time jobs like designing a poster or designing a story for $5 and paid me on time. For a few brands, I prepared giveaway/contest posters as well. After a few months, I started hosting contests/giveaways for the brands for a reasonable price. In this way, I have started counting my small wins.

Later I started applying for freelance social media manager jobs and landed my first client from the United Kingdom. I don't have any negative experiences in this process. I had only positive experiences with people and the platform. It mostly depends on how you react and with which kind of people you are building your network. My network helped me a lot in this process. So, building a network plays a vital role in your social media job hunt.

Has work been consistent for you?

For me, it is consistent, because whenever I ended up signing a contract with the client, I always focused on delivering good quality work and made sure that the client was happy with me and my work. This made me look more reliable and professional.

For any job, being professional is very important. For all my clients I have delivered a very good service and offered services that go above and beyond. Choosing a good client is important. You have to choose a good client who respects your time and pays you on time. But how do you find out whether a client is a good client or a bad client? And how to break up with a bad client? Here are the simple techniques I will tell you to identify this.

A good client always: 1. pays you on time 2. offers you training 3. is responsive 4. listens to you 5. offers you freedom of work.

A bad client: 1. demands more work from you but never increases your pay 2. delays payment 3. is never satisfied with your work and always complains 4. threatens to fire you 5. denies testimonials.

So, in this way, my journey was consistent because I had identified good clients and bad clients, eliminated bad clients from the list and continued with the good clients. Building a good client base is important as it gives you financial security and confidence.

Do you think people will increasingly need to look for work through social media?

It will increase. Covid-19 impacted all sectors and made it possible that most work can be done online. This increased the presence of people in social media communities. Almost all companies post their vacancies on their social media platforms. Most job-seekers search for jobs by building their profiles on social media platforms.

If you take another popular social networking platform, many groups specifically started for job-seekers and professionals. On a popular photo and video sharing platform, many freelancers are searching for jobs and successfully finding them. In the future also, this percentage will increase. Most companies and freelancing platforms ask you to give the link of your social media profile when there is a job interview. Also, social media is a good platform to showcase your original talent and build relationships with people, network, and keep you updated regarding the job trends. That's why many job-seekers are preferring to look for jobs through social media.

Every company would like to set up their profile on social media regularly posting about the company updates. This gesture is very helpful for job-seekers when they search for a job through social media and they can know the company updates at a glance. Traditional job-hunting will consume more time and is less successful when compared to job-searching through social media.

A word of wisdom for someone looking to get their first job on any social media platform

Try it until you succeed. Keep trying and keep moving forward. Count your small wins. Gain inspiration from other people. Look at their achievements. Get inspired by other job-seekers. Collaborate with brands. Build a network. Grow it regularly. Create social media profiles and manage them. Never get disappointed.

The first step to follow is to showcase your work on social media. It doesn't matter which social media platform you choose; you should publish your work. Only then will they come to know about your work. If you are a writer, start a blog and start publishing all your articles. If you are a photographer, start an account on a photo sharing social media platform and keep posting your photographs.

Build followers slowly. Interact with people. Keep sending cold messages and comments to brands and businesses. Offer them free services at the initial stages and give them quality work. Then they will spread the word about your skill and consider you for other jobs. Be consistent and considerate. Never lose your patience. Ask for referrals within your network. Try to participate in contests/giveaways hosted by the brands. It will increase your profile visibility. Offer free-of-charge services.

All these activities surely will help you land your first job through social media. If you want to get a job on social media, you should be active on social media.

The Hard Road of a Freelancer

Sovran Hoti - Albania

My name is Sovran Hoti. I've completed studies in English language and literature, earning a bachelor's degree and an associate's degree in this field. I have successfully found jobs on all kinds of platforms, but when I first started freelancing the first job I secured was on a popular freelancing platfrom. I ended up on this platform through my cousin, who has been using it for years now. When she first talked to me about it I was skeptical as I had no previous knowledge of this platform, and when I did, I was even more terrified of the thought of failing to deliver the work and getting myself into trouble.

I started using the online freelancing platform, and it took me some time to get used to how things operate, and what I can contribute the most to. I took it slowly, figuring out what I could do, what I couldn't, and whether I could learn. I started checking online videos for beginners on how I could obtain different skills for different apps that I didn't have any prior experience with. Every day I would learn a new skill (and still do), and things started getting easier after that. This has been life-changing for me and my career.

Was it difficult to get a job using social media?

The first couple of weeks were really tough for me when I started. Several weeks went by and I still hadn't secured any job. The first week, I didn't even get any responses or messages to discuss whether someone wanted to offer me work or not. I was investing money in buying connects, and then I would have to invest again because I wasn't getting anywhere. It was quite stressful and frustrating, as I quit my day-job to give this freelancing opportunity a shot. Then when I got my first job, the client didn't like my work and I had to refund her. I felt desperate after that. But everyday I would learn a new skill, I would learn different apps, and I would check where I needed improvement, and where I could polish my CV, experience, and skills.

A couple of weeks after the disaster with my first client I landed a job as a virtual assistant for a client and his company. I had zero experience, but he was willing to take a chance on me. I ended up working for him all of last year, doing content writing assignments, email, social media, and website tasks. The client was really patient with me and would give me extra time in finishing my assignments, and I was under no pressure. So, after that it became a very positive experience for me. I still stress now and then, but not so much now.

Has work been consistent for you?

I would say all in all it has been consistent work for me, especially last year. 2021 was a crazy year for me, as it was really my first year starting out in freelancing, and it has been so rewarding for me and my career. After the freelancing platform, I started using every app I could to get jobs. I got a lot of projects out of many popular social media platforms, by leaving what I work on my info. I grew both as a person and as a freelancer. During the end of 2021 I took a break to continue my studies, getting my associate's degree in English abroad, and I took some time off from freelancing during that period.

I have to admit that after finishing my studies, when I decided to take on more jobs this year it has been a struggle, as I had been out of the loop for a while and it took me some time to get my foot in again. I was not getting the jobs I wanted, and I had trouble with catching on some of the skills I had known but had forgotten, and also trying to catch up to learning new skills and new apps to enhance myself. But I guess I am on the path to getting up there again.

Do you think people will increasingly need to look for work through social media?

I think it will increase. The reason I say this is because I have seen it myself. If you are willing to learn, to take on new training, to be motivated, dedicated, and patient, jobs will eventually come to you. As you progress with each project and receive good feedback, your profile will increase. With the skills you learn each new day, your horizon will span various different areas, which will make it possible for you to obtain jobs that you had no idea that you could even do.

If you are persistent enough, decisive, and willing to learn, there is nothing that will get in your way. Make sure to promote your projects and your skills on every social media platform possible. You can never know when the next job will turn up, but when it does, you have the skills, the mindset, and the dedication to be ready for that job. Use all kinds of platforms. Even though you might not be getting projects on one or the other, do not give up, keep applying on all of them. You may be surprised that you might even get projects from platforms where you might not expect any results.

A word of wisdom for someone looking to get their first job on any social media platform

Do not give up. It is such a cliché saying this, but it is so true. It took me weeks to get my first client - weeks of investing money and money in connection credits on some platforms, money I did not have, and not getting anything. I applied on dozens of job applications, and I had no responses. And when I got my first client, he did not like my work, but I didn't give up.

The next client I secured turned out to be a long-term client for whom I worked for the rest of the year. That upped my profile, and the offers just kept coming. Also, learn new skills, even if you are not receiving any work, it is important that you learn new skills and new apps. You never know when it is going to come in handy.

Be open to new opportunities, training, courses, and experiences. You will be rewarded for it, sooner or later. Most importantly, be patient! Patience will go a long way, and it makes you grow as a person, and will help your career. Set lower goals, do not start out big at first. Set little things you can accomplish, and you can grow from there.

Afterword

As I read through all these accounts, I realize that not much has changed over time. The mindset of the job-hunter and the behaviors of employers, whether good or bad, have not changed with time. The only difference is that we use different tools, wear different clothes and show off different hair styles. No matter what platform we use for job hunting today, yesterday or in the future, the concepts are the same.

From the employer's perspective, it's about finding the right person for the job and from the job-seeker's perspective it's about demonstrating that they are the right person for the job. Processes such as interviews, checking references and testimonies, combing through portfolios are still tools used to match the right person to the job.

If you are reading this book today as a job-seeker, I want to encourage you. Finding the first job or in fact any job can be very difficult but it's not impossible, you just need to stand out from the rest of the pack. Find all your good qualities and amplify them, communicate with your prospective employer wholeheartedly and deliver the best work that you can.

I have been an employer, an employee and also a freelancer. As a freelancer I have had my fair share of small $5 jobs that take ages to complete, and today as I am writing this I have a top-rated freelancer badge on a popular freelancing website. As an employee, one of my first jobs after graduation was an hour's drive once a week to do a job that I didn't enjoy. Six years afterwards, I became an employer.

No matter what your situation is, don't give up, be creative in your approach, and take small steps towards your goal. Today I wrote this book to encourage you in your job seeking journey, so hopefully one day you can also encourage someone else towards getting their first job.

If you enjoyed this book you can visit our website to read many more stories.

arthurlee.com.au

More Titles to come!

www.ingramcontent.com/pod-product-compliance
Lightning Source LLC
Chambersburg PA
CBHW051538240526
45465CB00027B/689